DINNER AT LAS HERAS

LUCIANA JAZMÍN CORONADO
Translated from the Spanish by
ALLISON A. DEFREESE

C&R Press
Conscious & Responsible

All Rights Reserved

Printed in the United States of America

First Edition
1 2 3 4 5 6 7 8 9

Selections of up to two pages may be reproduced without permission. To reproduce more than two pages of any one portion of this book, write to C&R Press publishers John Gosslee and Andrew Ibis.

Cover art by Alsira Monforte Baz, Leer los
          Escombros /Read the Rubble
          (acrylic, charcoal and counting on canvas. 80x50cm)

Copyright ©2024 Luciana Jazmín Coronado and Allison A. deFreese
ISBN 978-1-949540-55-0

C&R Press
Conscious & Responsible
crpress.org

For discounted purchases, please contact: C&R Press sales@crpress.org

The Spanish language versions of these poems were originally published by Valparaíso Ediciones (Granada, Spain, 2016). This chapbook contains selected poems, in translation, from Luciana Jazmín Coronado's original poetry manuscript Catacombs/ Catacumbas.

The poems in this collection won the I Premio Hispanoamericano de Poesía de San Salvador/San Salvador's I Hispano-American Prize for Poetry (in the original, Spanish language), an international literary award organized by the San Salvador's Secretary of Culture (El Salvador).

TABLE OF CONTENTS

Dinner at Las Heras . . . 7

The Seam . . . 8

The Bomb . . . 9

I Am the Alchemist . . . 10

The Bear . . . 11

Rice Crispy Treats . . . 13

My Mother in the Kitchen . . . 14

The Secret . . . 15

The Lilac Nightgown . . . 16

The Garden . . . 17

The Chest Filled with Flowers . . . 18

The Surrender . . . 19

Brother . . . 20

The Bride . . . 21

Acknowledgements . . . 23

About the Author . . . 24

About the Translator . . . 26

DINNER AT LAS HERAS

Dinner at Las Heras

Las Heras 3847

DINNER AT LAS HERAS

an enormous flower
is growing under the table
as we eat dinner
its petals absorb
the shadowy voice
of my father's wife
the flower is near
I hide it
between my legs
it is a wild lily
I say nothing
I lose my color
from loss of blood
my father doesn't notice

Papa, let's run into the wind together,
play on the sun-bleached swing set
that used to be ours
but no . . .
dinner is served
I am dried out—
the flower keeps growing larger, overflowing
a living lamp
it frightens the whole household
she stops eating
I have lost
my insides
instead of dying
I decide
to connect my navel
to the flower's stem
as I gaze at my plaster family

THE SEAM

I pricked her lips with the pin
she remained anesthetized
sleeping at my father's side
stiff as the base
of a windmill
I enjoyed stitching up
her lips:
her blood didn't run
a perfect mask
took shape—
on the verge of preforming a ritual
later I watched my father,
a newly captured bear
come unraveled
on the white sheets

his mouth opening
with every breath
then I left
I was smaller
than the moon
on the doorstep

THE BOMB

my little brother and I
weren't expecting the bomb
but it has fallen
I see you
lying on the shattered glass—
all that remains:
a few thoughts
floating past, hidden behind the flames
the room is in ruins
the time there:
a morning glory in the sun
lilies will not blossom in this house
there will be no music

Hermanito, little one:
I saw a light before I felt the explosion—
it was the fragments of ocean
embedded in our heads

I AM THE ALCHEMIST

when Papa leaves me
he dies

then comes back to life
he is a night flower
his petals elongate
like thick banknotes
he embraces me
leaving me in shadow

I kill my father
then revive him
I am his alchemist

He must die in the wind
I've already created
several mutations of him—
in the remains, I find gemstones

Papa must die
turn to stone
stop being a panther:
no to feline eyes, no to cunning

Papa no longer exists
because he turned into a tree
from so much lying
then they sewed his mouth closed

THE BEAR

I used to sleep in the utility room
with a little stuffed bear
when I visited you, Papa.
it was the only toy there
and out of pity for the bear
I gave him your name: Daniel

Daniel hurts, Papa,
he is alive in me.
Daniel is sweet
but a carnivore inside
his pain is like the winter wind
biting my eyelashes

it hurts, Papa, Daniel,
your mirror inside me
a sculpture of salt
he hurts, Papa
but I don't bleed
I left my deepness
at the mouth of the well
your old face with its lines
and your spider web eyes
frighten me, Papa
what is inside me hurts
without a sense of touch
Papa, I have said
you will never see me again.
I will recite these words
until I sense you are dead
in the end, every word I speak
unbinds your web

casts your strands further from me.
Father of wind
you may be waiting for this poem
in your paleness
I will mark
your coffin
with chalk
I will embroider your clothes
I will create words
in your mouth
with these poems
I will enter softly, Papa
so as not to disturb you

RICE CRISPY TREATS

Papa brought rice crispy treats
clouds from last night's leftovers

Papa made me swallow lunch
while ballet music played

Papa, don't try to make me eat
or you'll find my books flying off the shelves
you'll see me hide inside stories
spin my toys in the air
sort my swords

Papa brought my remains
in a box
They are drawings of confinement
in bright colors

Papa, Papa! Didn't you see the polar bears?
Didn't you notice my nets spreading?

I embrace my brothers now
I medicate them and protect them
like a strong father would

as I consider what you took
what you never gave me

MY MOTHER IN THE KITCHEN

each day in the kitchen
my mother crochets a faith,
scouring the pages of books
for answers
to what has ceased to be
though she conceals them
her wrinkles are lovely,
giving me glimpses
of the years deferred
while she raised me,
of the hours spent feeding me
and teaching me to speak
I wait for my mother
as she crochets a faith
a kettle whistling ceaselessly
as day becomes night
she remains there
surrounded by books,
distant
as the motionless moons
on her nightgown
she continues past midnight
without having eaten;
with effort she boils the zucchini
imagining a raincoat
hides her
from all that is to come
I can take her hand
and tell her everything is alright,
that year after year
she had been leaving me
a basement full of stars

THE SECRET

for a week
after learning
that her boyfriend
of all those years had passed away
in a nursing home
my grandmother kept quiet
she kept this secret
along with the others
I dream of opening the top of her head
once she's gone
and looking through
all the thoughts
hidden away in those little boxes
sorted according to type
like tiny gemstones or jewelry
I dream
of uncovering her treasure chests
and finally accepting
that certain things
are never ours

THE LILAC NIGHTGOWN

in the mirror
I catch a glimpse
of my grandmother's fallen breasts
as she lifts her arms
to let the pastel nightgown
fall over her, covering her body
from a distance she seems to be diving
into a field of lilacs
once dressed,
she comes over and hugs me
pressing her withered
stalwart body against mine
and says
I will always, always be with you
she swallows
and I know she's holding back tears
she tells me
all about her beautiful nightgowns
shows me the wardrobe
overflowing with her clothes
I will be with you
I imagine myself grown up
playing with my own children
as she waves at me
from the window
covered head to toe in lavender

THE GARDEN

The garden was steeped
in a dark substance
when I arrived;
the spiders were white
in comparison
I did a double take
not expecting
to find it so close by
nor to lose my sight
in the darkness
I drew near, holding the scissors
and severed a juicy aloe leaf,
its glistening petroleum
flowed out
with the overwhelming scent of saints
Slowly I licked
a drop of aloe off my finger
a flock birds
took flight from my tongue
now I've reached the other side
I light a match
I can still babble language

THE CHEST FILLED WITH FLOWERS

if I no longer see you
in the garden
if you stop trimming the buds
on the rosebush Grandpa planted
if I stop looking at
your hands
with their large freckles,
extending towards the sun
or watching you sit down
to rinse your legs
as the blood gathers
in your swollen feet
then:
how much longer
will it be until
the garden goes into hiding
and a chest filled with blue flowers
illuminates what's under the soil?

THE SURRENDER

I clean her body
slowly
as if not to hurt her
I comb my grandmother
like a doll
silence beats
against the wreaths of flowers
one sob and then another
stitching a dress of droplets,
the morning dew
from La Lucila del Mar
I entrust her to the sun
and storms
and wipe clean
her wooden box
she is the only one I will pray for
the rest of this will dissipate
the scent of maté and pastries
that once filled the house,
the plants
that for years she tended and watered
until her hands
froze in mid-air
a drop
falling
without reaching
the ground

BROTHER

I hear you
across the atmospheres
when through the seasons
you tune your harp at times
when what silenced you
takes pity on your lips
and if wind and ocean
can no longer mouth a sound
to us it makes no difference
we still harbor love
like those ships
that return to port
after years at sea

THE BRIDE

My mother warns me
that Grandma has awakened
from death,
taken a shower
and put on a dress
over her naked body
together we run to the stairs,
watch her descend slowly
between the yellow marble balusters,
a bride
extinguishing her flame
at the altar,
the face emaciated
the lips red
halfway down
I give her a hug
You are beautiful,
I tell her,
and the world
can do nothing about it.
she smiles
like a paper girl
ready for her trip

ACKNOWLEDGEMENTS

The title of the book in your hands is a reference to a poem from the first section of Luciana Jazmín Coronado's *Catacombs/Catacumbas*, winner of the I Premio Hispanoamericano de la Poesía de San Salvador/ San Salvador's I Hispano-American Prize for Poetry. Each section or "catacomb" of that book refers to a different address in Buenos Aires (either real or imaginary) where the poet spent a fragment of her childhood. I am grateful to the following publications in which my English translations of selected poems from this chapbook have previously appeared, including:

Columbia Journal, "The Seam" and "The Bear"
Crazyhorse/swamp pink, "Dinner at Las Heras"
Gulf Coast: A Journal of Literature and Fine Arts, "The Bride" and "The Chest Filled with Flowers"

Rain Magazine, "The Garden" and "The Secret"

ABOUT THE AUTHOR

Luciana Jazmín Coronado was born in Buenos Aires in 1991 and holds a Bachelor of Arts from the University of Buenos Aires. She has published three books of poetry, *La insolación/Sunstroke* (Viajero Insomne, 2014), *Catacumbas / Catacombs* (Valparaíso, 2016), winner of San Salvador's I Hispano-American Prize for Poetry, and Los hijos *Imperfectos/Imperfect Children* (RIL, 2023). She has been awarded artists grants from the Antonio Gala Foundation for Young Creators (Córdoba, Spain, 2017) and the Writers Residency from UNESCO and University of Granada (Granada, Spain, 2019), among others. Her poems have been translated into several languages and published in international anthologies and literary journals. She currently lives in Tarragona, Spain.

Luciana Jazmín Coronado

ABOUT THE TRANSLATOR

Allison A. deFreese's translations of Luciana Jazmín Coronado's poetry appear in *Boulevard*, *Pacifica*, and *swamp pink*, and were a finalist in Poetry International's annual chapbook competition. Allison has translated books by other Argentinian writers including Carolina Esses' *Winter Season* (Entre Ríos Books, 2023) and María Negroni's *Elegy for Joseph Cornell* (Dalkey Archive Press, 2020).

ALLISON A. DEFREESE

C&R PRESS CHAPBOOKS

C&R Press hosts two chapbook selection periods from June to September and November to March each year. The Summer Tide Pool and Winter Soup Bowl Chapbook Series are open to new and established writers in poetry, fiction, essay and other creative writing genres.

2023 SUMMER TIDE POOL
The Consolation of Geometry by Alice Campbell Romano

2023 WINTER SOUP BOWL
Dinner at Las Heras Allison A. deFreese's translation from the Spanish of Luciana Jazmín-Coronado

2022 SUMMER TIDE POOL
The Ice Beneath the Earth by Brian Ascalon Roley

2022 WINTER SOUP BOWL
tommy noun by Maurya Kerr

2021 SUMMER TIDE POOL
Rocketflower by Matthew Meade

2021 WINTER SOUP BOWL
We Face the Tremenedous Meat on the Teppan by Naoko Fujimoto

2020 WINTER SOUP BOWL
My Roberto Clemente by Rick Hilles

2019 SUMMER TIDE POOL
Inside the Orb of an Oracle by Dannie Ruth

2019 WINTER SOUP BOWL
The Magical Negro Reveals His Secret by Gabriel Green

2018 SUMMER TIDE POOL
Yell by Sarah Sousa

2018 WINTER SOUP BOWL
Paleotemptestology by Bertha Crombet

White Boys from Hell by Jeffrey Skinner

2017 SUMMER TIDE POOL
Atypical Cells of Undetermined Significance by Brenna Womer

2017 WINTER SOUP BOWL
Heredity and Other Inventions by Sharona Muir

On Inaccuracy by Joe Manning

2016 SUMMER TIDE POOL
Cuntstruck by Kate Northrop

Relief Map by Erin M. Bertram

Love Undefined by Jonathan Katz

2016 WINTER SOUP BOWL
Notes from the Negro Side of the Moon by Earl Braggs

A Hunger Called Music: A Verse History in Black Music by Meredith Nnoka

Milton Keynes UK
Ingram Content Group UK Ltd.
UKHW031352011224
451755UK00004B/367